# Hello, Friend!

## by Katy Black

Glenview, Illinois • Boston, Massachusetts • Chandler, Arizona
Upper Saddle River, New Jersey

"Hello, friend!"
Friends are special.
It is important to have friends.
It is important to be a good friend.

How do you make friends?
Say hello to someone new.
"Hi, what is your name?"
"Do you want to play soccer?"

What does a good friend do?
A good friend helps you.
A good friend talks with you.
A good friend shares.
A good friend cares.

How can you be a good friend?
Help a friend who needs something.
Ask a sad friend what is wrong.

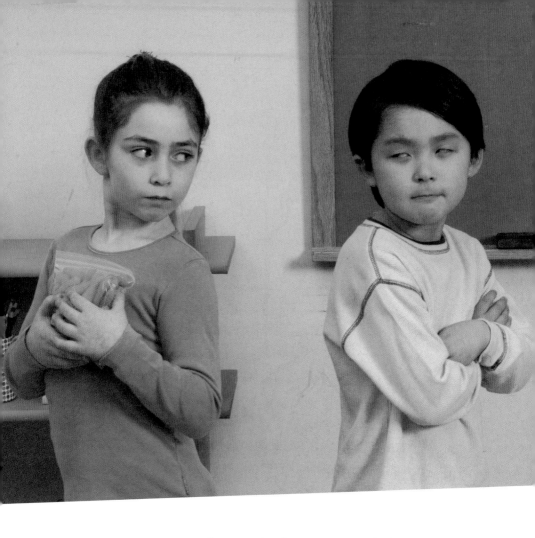

Sometimes friends have problems.
What can you do?
Listen to your friend. Try to share.
Say you are sorry if you were not nice.

This is how friends can fix a problem.
"I want that snack!"
"I want it!"
"Can we share?"
"Yes, we can."

| If | Then |
|---|---|
| you want a new friend, | smile and say hello. |
| you have a problem with a friend, | try to fix it. |
| you care for a friend, | ask if you can help. |

How do you feel with a good friend?
You feel happy.
A good friend makes you feel good!